# AGAPE

## The Love Of God

"BY THIS SHALL ALL MEN KNOW THAT YOU ARE MY DISCIPLES IF YOU HAVE AGAPE"
– JOHN 13:35

# AGAPE
## The Love Of God

## JOE HUEBSCHER

ReadersMagnet, LLC

# Contents

# Introduction

WHEN I WAS A TEENAGER, I BECAME A Christian and immediately developed a hunger for the Word of God. I had tried to read the Bible before I became a Christian but could not. I would read one of the Gospels and then lose interest as I started a second one. I just could not read very far at all. However, once I became a Christian, I read the entire Bible from cover to cover in just several months.

I also began memorizing passages, both in the Old Testament and the New. But I also wanted very much to understand them. The word "faith" was the first problem I encountered. It appeared to be a word used in working magic. Just how could faith uproot a tree or move a mountain? I had never seen nor even heard of such a thing outside of the Bible or in fairy tales. But I also realized that Jesus was not an ordinary person. He was God's Son and so had special power. His disciples had been especially chosen and so they received special power from Him.

One word really did bother me, the word "love." When asked what was the greatest commandment, Jesus answered by saying, "You shall love the LORD your God with all your heart, with all your soul, and with all your mind. This is the first and great commandment. And the second is like it: You shall love your neighbor as yourself" (Matthew 22:37-39).[1] My thought was, "This is unrealistic; it's actually impossible. Love is an emotion, and no one can force his emotions to do anything." After pondering on the

---

1     All quotations of Scripture are taken from the NKJV.

matter for some time, I put the whole subject on a mental shelf; but I also continued to gather bits of information from here and there and to store them up. I did not lose interest. The subject has followed me throughout my life. I am no longer a teenager, but the subject of love has continued with me. You may even guess what was the subject of my final paper in graduate school.

The main word we are concerned with is αγάπη (agapē), translated "love". I will only refer to it in this writing with English letters so that it will be seen as "*agape.*" It occurs in the New Testament one hundred sixteen times, always a noun and always translated "love."

Another word, αγαπάω (*agapaō*), is built on the same stem and often used in the same way, but is also used in a number of other ways as well. It is a verb and it too is usually translated "love." It occurs in the New Testament one hundred forty-two times. In English one word, "love," serves both as a noun and a verb. A person must decide from the context how it is being used. In Greek they are two different words and though built on the same stem may not always mean the same thing. The earliest date that the noun can be found in all literature is in the Greek translation of the Old Testament, usually called the Septuagint, which was produced in about the third century before Christ. I have discovered a number of references where it is found earlier in Greek literature than the third century before Christ, but they have all been disputed as to the date in which they were actually written. The translators of the Septuagint appear to have been the originators of the noun "*agape.*"

There is no clear example of the word in secular Greek literature prior to the second century after Christ. This is well into the Christian era. Hermann Creamer thinks that the translators of the Septuagint were the originators of the word. The references there are twelve—Ecclesiastes 9:1 and 6; Jeremiah 2:2; and the Song of Solomon 2:4, 5, 7; 3:5; 5:8; 7:6; 8:4, 6, and 7. From this list it is very evident that the word had a very different meaning than when the New Testament writers used it. There it generally occurs in a sexual context.

In the Gospels, only Jesus used the word *agape* and only when referring to Himself or to His Father. The Gospel writers themselves used the Greek word phile.

Paul is the writer who uses the word *agape* the most in the New Testament. He wrote First Corinthians, probably in early 54 A.D. That book contains the "love" chapter—13; which is a description of the word *agape*. All the other writers of the New Testament then followed Paul's example and included the word *agape* in their writings.

# The Importance of Agape

PAUL BROUGHT THE WORD *AGAPE* TO LIFE WHEN he wrote First Corinthians 13. He introduced the chapter by calling it "a more excellent way." In the first three verses of this chapter, he shows the importance of *agape* to the quality of a person's life. A person's communication ability is mentioned first: "Though I speak with the tongues of men and of angels but have not love" (*agape*) my speech is of little value. I am just making a noise. Secondly, there is no profit even of having a spiritual gift of performing miracles without *agape*, according to verse two. In verse three, even the gift of giving is of no profit without the motivation that comes from *agape*.

On one particular day in Jesus' life, the leaders of Israel attempted to trip Him up. They were not very successful, for when a Sadducee asked Him about the resurrection of the dead (Matthew 22:23-28), Jesus easily diffused his argument. Immediately, a Pharisee who was also a lawyer asked Him what the greatest commandment is. Again, with ease his argument was discredited, for Jesus had a ready answer, quoting from Deuteronomy, "You shall love the LORD your God with all your heart, with all your soul, and with all your mind. This is the first and great commandment." Being the first commandment did not mean "first" historically, but rather "first" in importance.

But how could this be so? I have heard for years that the chief end of man is "to glorify God and to enjoy Him forever." If such were true, a person would think that the greatest commandment is to glorify God, but this is not a commandment at all. Jesus said that the greatest commandment is to have *agape* toward God.

In the first chapter of Genesis, God makes a very definite, clear statement regarding what He was about to do. He said, "Let us make man in our image, after our likeness" (Genesis 1:26). An earlier verse in the chapter depicted God creating the universe and everything in it. He pronounced each item "good," which indicated that He had a plan or purpose that He was following very closely so that at the end of the chapter He pronounced everything "very good." It certainly appears that verse twenty-six is God's purpose statement. It states exactly what He planned or proposed to do, which makes this verse extremely important. IMAGING GOD then would be the chief end of mankind.

Paul referred to Genesis chapter one in Romans 8:28 when he stated that "all things work together for good." He used the Greek word, πρόθεσις for "purpose." This word literally means "to lay it all out in advance." So, God had a plan laid out in advance for all that He made. And all these things that God made, He made for those who had *agape* for Him and those who would bear His image.

This truth fits very well with John's statement that "God is *agape*" (I John 4:8). Putting it this way, *agape* is at the very heart of God. Furthermore, this puts *agape* in a different category than "God is Holy." As a noun, *agape* shows God's very basic character. The word "holy" is an adjective and can only describe what He is like.

John also tells us that *agape* is so characteristic of God that, if a person does not show any *agape*, it is because he does not know God. Every true Christian demonstrates *agape* at various times and to some extent. As we reflect God's image, *agape* will be seen in our lives.

Now, if John is correct when he writes his first epistle, that only Christians experience *agape* and that every Christian demonstrates *agape* to some extent, then it is easy to understand why secular Greek society would not have a word to express it since this practice was not in their culture. A new word needed to be invented for Christians, and it would need to become a part of God's Word.

John, the disciple closest to Jesus, was chosen to show how essential *agape* is to the very nature of God, when He penned "God is *agape*." Furthermore, a second person, Paul, who was multicultural, possessing a keen insight and much zeal, was needed to explain how to live it and to exemplify it with his own life in order to impress upon each of us Christians today the importance of *agape* in our lives.

With that in mind, let us look at *agape*.

# Agape Defined

"JESUS GAVE HIMSELF." FIVE TIMES THIS IS RECORDED: Galatians 1:4, "Who gave Himself for our sins"; Galatians 2:20, "Who loved me and gave Himself for me"; Ephesians 5:25, "even as Christ also loved the church and gave Himself for it"; I Timothy 2:6, "Who gave Himself a ransom for all"; and Titus 2:14, "Who gave Himself for us that He might redeem us and purify unto Himself a peculiar people zealous of good works." Also, II Corinthians 8:5 tells of the Churches of Macedonia giving themselves: "But first gave their own selves to the Lord and unto us." The best definition for *agape* love that I have found is "giving oneself for the good of the other."

Besides *agape*, there are other Greek words translated "love." Φιλέω (*phileo*), φίλος (*philos*), and φιλία (*philia*) are three words translated as love into English. These three words have the same stem. The first is a verb which occurs twenty-five times in the New Testament. Twenty-two of these times it is translated "love" and the remaining three times "kiss." The second word, "philos," occurs twenty-nine times and is always translated "friend." The noun, "philia", occurs only in James 4:4 and is translated "friendship." These words denote a natural affection along with one's emotions. These are the only other Greek words in the New Testament translated as "love."

Ερος (*eros*), another Greek word, does not occur in the New Testament. It generally means to desire passionately or is used to describe sexual passion. It does not express a desire for the good of the other but rather a desire of the other for oneself.

# The Source of Agape

JOHN PRESENTS THE DEITY OF CHRIST WHO, AS God's Son, declares God's *agape*: "…that you may believe that Jesus is the Christ, the Son of God; and that believing you may have life through His name" (John 20:31). John strongly emphasizes that God is the source of all *agape* and that the Son mediates that love. No clause could more strongly emphasize the source of *agape* than "God is love" (I John 4:8 and 18). The setting of the verse, I John 4:7-10, makes the statement "*agape* is of God" more completely:

> "Beloved let us love one another, for love is of God; and everyone who loves is born of God and knows God. He who does not love does not know God, for God is love. In this the love of God was manifested toward us, that God has sent His only begotten Son into the world, that we might live through Him. In this is love, not that we loved God, but that He loved us, and sent His Son to be the propitiation for our sins."

The whole context emphasizes that "*agape* is of God," and anyone who has *agape* is born of God, or in the words of John 3:7, "is born again." A person who is not born again cannot have *agape*; it is foreign to Him. This truth appears to be emphasized strongly by John and is probably the reason why the word is not found in secular Greek before this time.

# Agape in The New Testament

THE SYNOPTIC GOSPELS ARE MATTHEW, MARK, AND LUKE. As one would expect, neither the noun, *agape*, nor the verb, *agapao*, is mentioned very much in the Gospels. The only truth these three books contribute to the concept of *agape* is the idea of loving one's enemy. One expects the absence of the words *agape* and *agapao* when one realizes that these words were not common at the time of Christ, nor did they contribute to the purpose of the Synoptic Gospel writers. Their main use was the testimonies they gave of the life of Christ. The differences in the writer's ages, nationalities, vocations and cultural backgrounds are of tremendous value as they testify of the life of Christ. These differences highlight the actions of Jesus with the interests of each writer. All three Gospels, however, tell of Jesus' encounter with a group of Herodians, Sadducees and Pharisees who attempted to trip Him up by asking which was the great commandment in the law. Jesus responded by saying, "you shall love…" With His answer, Christ places *agape* for God above all other obligations.

# Instances When Agape Is Directed Toward God

SEVERAL OBSERVATIONS CAN BE MADE CONCERNING THIS COMMAND to love God. First, it is taken from Deuteronomy 6:4-5, by Christ and placed above the Ten Commandments. The Ten Commandments had priority in Jewish culture and the Pharisee referred to them in his question to Christ. However, in answering, Christ quoted another commandment, rather than any one of the ten, though his choice was probably equally as familiar.

This command implies absolute devotion and submission to God as well as adoration for Him as the basic motivation for one's life. It contains the same idea that Christ expressed in the Sermon on the Mount: "But seek first the kingdom of God and His righteousness, and all these things shall be added to you" (Matthew 6:33). *Agape* must be expressed, and since man cannot see God, and God is so far from being His equal that he cannot even do God a favor, then the only avenues left by which he can demonstrate *agape* is through faith, devotion, adoration, and submission. Faith is crucial. It shows trust. By devotion to God, a person realizes that God constitutes the highest good. By adoring God, a person demonstrates enjoyment of God as the highest good. By submission to Him, a person allows God to produce God-like characteristics in his own life and the same characteristics in the lives of others.

Also, this command leaves no room for the love of any enemy or any master opposed to God. Christ stated that only two alternatives existed: "no man can serve two masters: for either he will hate the one, and love the other; or else he will be loyal to the one, and despise the other. You cannot serve God and mammon" (Matthew 6:24). If one has *agape* towards God with all his heart, and with all his soul, and with all his mind, no room remains for him to have *agape* for anyone opposed to God, anything different from God, or any one toward which God does not have *agape*, except as a means to win them to the Lord. This concept remains consistent throughout both the New and Old Testaments. In many places, such as Exodus 2:5, 34:14, Deuteronomy 4:24, and II Corinthians 11:2, one reads that God is a jealous God, and to love another in His place is idolatry and spiritual adultery.

Though Jesus gives this most important command to have *agape* for the Lord God, He also warns of three enemies that oppose *agape* and against which one must continually war: mammon, pride, and pleasures. Mammon is a common Aramaic word for riches. A specific warning concerning it occurs in both Matthew 6:24 and Luke 16:13 in addition to less specific warnings throughout the Gospels. A love for mammon quickly robs a person of his love for God. Pride is continually met and battled in the Synoptics in the self-righteousness and hypocrisy of the scribes and Pharisees, though only once specifically named in Mark 7:22. It displays itself in selfishness, which appears to be the exact opposite of *agape*. Selfishness seeks the temporal good of a person, while *agape* seeks the eternal. Pleasure constitutes the enjoyment of temporal things in opposition to the enjoyment of the highest good. Consequently, it is condemned in the parable of the rich fool who completely ignored God in his philosophy to eat, drink, and be merry (Luke 12:16-21 and Matthew 6:25-34).

# Agape for One's Neighbor

The parable of the good Samaritan (Luke 10:25–37) also uses the word *agape*. It arises from the second great commandment that a person is to show the same *agape* to his neighbor as he does to himself. With this parable Christ answers specifically the question, "And who is my neighbor?" asked by the lawyer to justify himself.

*Agape* occurs in the parable when a Samaritan, an enemy of the Jews, discovers a Jew stripped and beaten by thieves and left for dead along the roadway. Without considering the purpose of his interrupted journey nor the time lost in his care for the victim of the thieves, he binds up the wounds of the man, (probably tearing up his own clothes to do so), pours oil and wine on the sores, and takes the man to an inn on his own mode of transportation and at the risk of being robbed and beaten himself. At the inn he takes care of the man who was robbed, and upon departing, he pays the innkeeper to continue caring for the man, promising to pay more if it is needed upon his return. Thus, true *agape* for one's neighbor demands a willingness to sacrifice one's own needs and rights, to give up certain comfort, to risk one's own life, and to pay the cost. In the parable, the neighbor was actually an enemy, and thus true *agape* demands this type of attitude toward all whom one might meet.

This action of the Samaritan, however, was not an act of general philanthropy. The one who is nearest to the one in need of help is the neighbor. The command to love one's neighbor as one's self eliminates all selfishness. Christ demands this sort of love of all who would follow Him.

# Agape for One's Enemy

THE COMMAND TO SHOW *AGAPE* TOWARDS ONE'S ENEMY occurs three times in the Synoptics (Matthew 5:44 Luke 6:27 and 6:35). This command does not occur in the Old Testament and constitutes an advancement in revelation. The Old Testament does, however, contain admonitions to hate. Hatred in itself is not wrong; but the object and motive of hatred determines its moral value. The hatred admonished in the Old Testament is a "righteous" hatred toward evil (Psalm 97:10; 119:104; and Amos 5:15) and as such, it becomes an ethical virtue. This hatred is not only to be directed toward evil in the abstract but also toward evildoers, that is, those who are enemies of God. It then becomes easy to rationalize and apply hatred to anyone a person does not like. Sense patriotism abounded in Palestine during the time of Christ; they had probably done this very thing. The commands to love one's enemies created the reaction of Christ to correct the whole atmosphere of hate He met on every hand.

The only way a child of God can show *agape* to his enemy is to do everything possible and in good taste to get one's enemy to obtain saving faith in Christ. Deeds of kindness are only means to this end - useful, but not acts of *agape* in themselves.

# Agape for Oneself

WHAT IS SELF-LOVE, AND DO THE FOLLOWING BIBLE verses forbid it? "For all seek their own, not the things which are Jesus Christ's" (Phil. 2:21); "Look not every man on his own things, but every man also on the things of others" (Phil. 2:4); "and that He died for all, that they which live should not henceforth live unto themselves, but unto Him which died for them, and rose again" (II Cor. 5:15).

*Agape* love is a deliberate choice of giving oneself for the good of another. If "good" is imaging God as Genesis 1:26 would indicate, then *agape* self-love would only improve my *agape* for others. As such, *agape* love for self is not forbidden. Rather, the verses above address selfishness.

The word "selfishness" itself does not occur in the Bible, though the action is often illustrated and is always condemned. An obvious instance of condemnation occurs in II Timothy 3:2, "for men shall be lovers of their own selves." The stem of this word is not *agape* but rather phile.

As God created us in His own image and is continuing to form us into that image, we, as Christians will find life most satisfying as we adopt the most basic characteristic of God, *agape*, as the most basic characteristic of ourselves—to give oneself for the good of the other, and all will take note that we are His disciples as we have *agape* one for another.

# The Example of Christ

*AGAPE* DEMANDS ACTIONS. MERE TALK ABOUT THE LOVE of God makes no sense unless it is applied to the lives of individuals. Jesus Christ is easily the supreme example of this.

Jesus manifested *agape* by His very presence on Earth in his incarnate state. He came "to seek and to save that which is lost" (Luke 19:10) and called others to join Him in this work for His Father. His entire life was dedicated to serving others, for He came "not to be ministered unto, but to minister, and to give His life a ransom for others" (Mark 10:45). As He traveled throughout Palestine, He restored sight to the blind, He restored mobility to the lame, He cleansed lepers, He restored hearing to the deaf, He raised the dead, and He preached the Gospel to the poor (Matthew 11:5).

In what way were these miracles of kindness acts of *agape*? The relief of physical suffering does not necessarily promote the highest good, although in some cases it may. Other suffering may even be the result of chastening from the Lord (Hebrews 12:4-11). Furthermore, if all relief of physical suffering worked for one's good, why did not Christ with one command end all such suffering? In Christ's answer to the disciples of John, He implies that His miracles of kindness were the fulfillment of prophecy. Because of the miracles Christ did perform, John should have known that He was the Messiah. The acceptance of this knowledge constitutes faith and produces eternal life (John 17:3). Even if a person did not realize that Christ's miracles of kindness were the fulfillment of prophecy, the miracles still were designed to produce faith and result in a person's highest good. As Christ saw the multitude with all its sickness and problems, he was moved with compassion because they "were scattered abroad, as sheep having no shepherd" (Matthew 9:36). He is the Good Shepherd who cares for the best interests of His sheep.

Christ rejected the popular demands for political leadership and an earthly kingdom but chose instead the role of a suffering servant who gave His life that others might be saved from eternal damnation. When despised and crucified, He did not revile his enemies or curse God, but motivated by *agape*, He prayed to His Father to "forgive them for they know not what they do" (Luke 23:34).

He often associated with sinners, though He had to withstand the wrath of the Pharisees to do so. Looking into evil hearts, He could see that only as a person realized his sinfulness would he seek a remedy. The publicans and sinners knew that they themselves had offended God and were condemned, and so they would more rapidly accept the forgiveness offered by Christ. The Pharisee, clothed in his self-righteousness, saw no such need.

God forgives the sins of only those who have a forgiving attitude (Matthew 6:15, 18:35) and will allow in heaven only those who do His will (Matthew 7:21). He even turned his back on the Lord Jesus when the sin of the world was upon Him on the cross (Matthew 27:46).

Neither does Jesus pamper those who live in sin. He will never allow workers of iniquity to abide in His presence (Matthew 7:23), and He was not afraid to pronounce the severest of woes upon cities, (Matthew 11:20-24) as well as upon people (Matthew 23:1-36) who stubbornly refused Him when He would have gathered them together "even as a hen gathers her chickens under her wings" (Matthew 23:37). Yet, to those who are willing to forsake their sin, the invitation remains to "come unto me, all you who labor and are heavy laden, and I will give you rest" (Matthew 11:28).

# The Parables of Christ

THE SUBJECT OF *AGAPE* SHOWS UP IN MANY of the parables. The parable on forgiveness (Matthew 18:21-35) recounts when Peter asked Christ how often he should forgive his brother who sins against him. Christ answered with the parable of a servant who was hopelessly in debt, yet when forgiven by his master, would not forgive one of his fellow servants. The parable shows that, though all God's servants are debtors to Him, He will freely forgive. But any servant who has been forgiven should in turn freely forgive any other who might sin against Him. Each servant is under obligation to treat a fellow servant in the same fashion as he has been treated by God—in love.

*Agape*, for one another is thus shown to be based upon God's *agape* by the words of the king, "Shouldest you not also have had compassion on your fellow servant, even as I had pity on you?" (verse 33). God demands that the recipients of His *agape* treat each other in harmony with His own character and actions.

Two other truths also appear in this parable. First, the size of the servant's debt was greater than he could then pay or would ever be able to pay, even as is true of each of God's servants who live on planet Earth today. Second, verse 32 shows that God's *agape* is sufficient to forgive all his servant's debt.

The parable of the vineyard in Matthew 21:33-46 gives two additional thoughts on *agape*. This parable concerns the housemaster who planted a vineyard and sent his servants to collect the fruits from it. The first thought revolves around the care which the housemaster gave to the vineyard by hedging it, building a tower, and digging a winepress, making a first-class piece of property which he loaned to the husbandman. The second is the housemaster's long suffering. He repeatedly sent his servants and even his own son before he destroyed those selfish and unjust men. God's *agape* has great endurance but is conditioned by love for His Son.

The parable of the marriage feast in Matthew 22:1-14 gives additional information. Christ tells of a king who invited certain ones to the wedding feast of his son. However, those invited refused the invitation of the King and showed their hostility by seizing his servants, insulting them, and even killing some. They rejected the king's love just as many reject God's *agape*. Then the king commanded his servants to "go into the highways, and as many as you find, invite to the wedding." The invitation was then open to all who would accept, even as is the invitation of *agape* today (John 3:16). But a condition needed to be met before one could participate in the king's wedding feast. The first ones who were invited, but refused, were destroyed and their city burnt, while the man without a wedding garment was bound hand and foot and cast into outer darkness. Thus, God's *agape* has certain limitations and cannot be separated from His holiness. Those invited by God are not required to accept, but are completely free to reject this offer of grace being extended to them. That person who accepts it, however, is required to wear Christ's robe of righteousness, the wedding garment.

The parables of the talents (Matthew 25:14-30) and of the pounds (Luke 19:11-27) are similar. They show the *agape* of God in giving to his servants. God, however, does not give for the sake of giving, but rather, calls each one who has received this gift to give an account as to what he has done with his gift. Each one who does well with His gift shall receive a reward.

The parable of the two debtors (Luke 7:41-42) illustrates that forgiveness from sin inspires true devotion to God. The one who was forgiven the most would in turn love Him the most. Though the actual statement occurs in I John, this parable illustrates perfectly that "we love Him because He first loved us."

In the parable of the barren fig tree (Luke 13:6-9), the Lord expects fruit, while an unproductive plant can expect nothing but judgment. *Agape* occurs in the delay in judgment and in the care given to the plant, which was dug about and fertilized. God holds off judgment until every opportunity for bearing fruit is exhausted, but then the fateful time will come.

The parable of the great supper in Luke 14:7-24 is very similar to that of the marriage feast in Matthew 22. It contributes to one's knowledge of God's *agape* by showing that, although expecting a response, it does not expect a recompense. It is for this reason that Christ teaches that "when you give a dinner or a supper, do not ask your friends, your brothers, your relatives, not your rich neighbors... but... invite the poor, the maimed, the lame, the blind: and you will be blessed; because they cannot repay you" (Luke 14:12-14).

The last three parables showing *agape* are related: the lost sheep, the lost coin, and the lost son. All occur in Luke 15, though the parable of the lost sheep also occurs in Matthew 18. The introductory statements, "For the Son of man has come to save that which was lost" (Matthew 18:11) and "The Pharisees and scribes complained, saying, this man receives sinners, and eats with them" (Luke 15:2) show that these parables were told for the express purpose of showing the nature of God's *agape*. The attitude of the sheep and the boy, who both deliberately went astray, would not arouse a phileo type of love in the shepherd and the father, but would rather offend them. However, because *agape* is being illustrated, the shepherd, the woman, and the father search diligently and endure great hardship, not for their own benefit, but for the benefit of that which is lost. The main point of the last parable centers on the character of the older brother who illustrates the Pharisees. They had been righteous, God-fearing, and law abiding throughout their lives and yet, the father apparently shows more love to his younger son, who illustrates the sinner, than to his older brother who illustrates the self-righteous Pharisees.

Since *agape* has a vital relationship to God and to Christ, one naturally expects the concept to appear in the parables. Of the eleven parables mentioned that show *agape*, all of them also include rebuke, judgment, and righteousness. God is so intensely interested in those who belong to Him that He gives His all, forgives their sins, invites and compels them to enter his fold, and lavishly bestows upon them blessing. But such love can never be severed from God's holiness and judgment upon sin. The *agape* of the parables demonstrates a moral love which demands a particular response from those who would reap its blessings.

# The Sermon on the Mount

THIS PORTION OF SCRIPTURE ABOUNDS WITH THE CONCEPT of *agape*. The Beatitudes could not proceed from any other characteristic of God but *agape*. Yet, these blessings are not thrown about indiscriminately wherever they might fall. God's blessings are guided by a moral principle and abide upon those who possess the qualities which characterize Himself. They are entirely selfless. Christ claimed the quality of "poor in spirit" when he said, "for I am meek and lowly in heart" (Matthew 11:28). The removal of pride is the first step toward salvation. Meekness is controlled strength, which Jesus claimed for Himself (Matthew 11:28). Christ possesses each quality mentioned in this portion of Scripture. Furthermore, many of these qualities have their counterpart in I Corinthians 13:4-7, Paul's descriptive chapter of *agape*. "Poor in spirit" corresponds to "not puffed up"; "mourn" corresponds to "does not rejoice in iniquity"; "meek" to "not behave rudely, is not easily provoked"; and "hunger and thirst after righteousness" to "rejoices in the truth."

Much of Matthew 5 concerns showing *agape* to other humans. By acting as salt and light, the Christian shows his *agape* to the unsaved and thereby brings glory to "your Father which is in heaven" as he brings others to a place where they too can be conformed to the image of God's Son. *Agape* does not seek to destroy one's brother nor hurt him in any way but seeks to live in harmony with him, and if need be, to be reconciled with Him. In domestic affairs, a man should be content with his own wife and not seek another or a divorce. One's attitude should always be that of giving, even when he might receive evil (verses 38-40) or whether it is companionship (verse 41), or whether it is that which a neighbor might need (verse 42). The chapter concludes by commanding *agape* for one's enemies. The final verse (48) shows perfection, a characteristic of God, to be *agape's* goal.

Chapter 6 of Matthew concerns selfishness, which is the result of one's own will choosing its own desires. A person who has *agape* does not show off in public with his alms, prayers, or fasting. Rather, he does these things in private to be seen of God alone on whom he depends. Neither does he lay up treasures for himself upon the Earth, but he seeks first the Kingdom of God and His righteousness (Matthew 6:33).

Chapter 7 begins by condemning those whose attitude is destructive by constant criticism of others, while their own lives manifest a neglect of living up to their own standards. *Agape* constantly seeks avenues of helpfulness rather than of destruction. But in its helpfulness, *agape* guards that which is holy and will not allow it to be given to the dogs (verse 6). Though God gives freely to His children who ask, His gifts are "good things" determined so by His own standards. God's actions constitute an example to His children that they ought to give only "good" things, doing to others as they would have others do to them (verses 11-12).

# Agape in James and Acts

JAMES DOES NOT USE THE WORD *AGAPE* IN his book, and *agapao* occurs only three times. The first instance occurs within a Beatitude that insinuates that the Christian who endures temptation is loved by God. The person who does endure temptation must, by the nature of temptation, be a spiritual person who desires those things that are eternal rather than temporal. This usage is, therefore, consistent with the definition: giving oneself for the good of the other. The other two references are likewise consistent. The first states that the ones showing *agape* to God have been promised an inheritance in the Kingdom. "Listen, my beloved brethren: Has God not chosen the poor of this world to be rich in faith and heirs of the kingdom which He promised to those who love Him?" (James 2:5) The second merely quotes the second great commandment: "You shall love your neighbor as yourself" and labels it the "Royal Law" (James 2:8)

The book of Acts contains neither *agape* nor *agapao*. Since it is a historical book written for the purpose of recording the early life of the church, it specifically relates the growth of the church in size and its spread geographically through the labors of the apostles Peter and Paul. Nevertheless, *agape* appears as the motive for the labors of those who bear the gospel.

One specific instance of the display of *agape* among Christians occurs in chapter two. These early believers had all things in common. Many of those having some wealth voluntarily sold their possessions and shared the proceeds with those in need. The behavior of Ananias and Sapphira, however, in lying concerning the amount they had brought to give, as told in chapter five, brought forth a severe warning against any selfish motive, resulting in the death of both.

Chapter 11 tells of another definite instance of the display of *agape* as a display of selfless love. It was occasioned by a famine in Judea. The Christians at Antioch, "every man according to his ability, determined to send relief unto the brethren who dwelt in Judea; which also they did." Paul's message to the Ephesian elders also, gives evidence of his *agape* since "for the space of three years" he "ceased not to warn everyone night and day with tears" (Acts 20:31).

# Agape and the Epistles of Paul

PAUL MENTIONS *AGAPE* IN EVERY ONE OF HIS Epistles and uses the word more than any other writer of the New Testament. The noun form, *agape*, occurs much more frequently (75 times), than does the verb form, *agapao* (34 times) and this frequency of the noun form is unique compared with all usage of the two words by any previous writer. Of the books already examined in the New Testament, the word *agape* does not occur at all in James, Mark, or Acts, and only once in Matthew and Luke. On further observation, it appears that each of the later books of the New Testament, those written after A.D. 60 with the exception of Mark, uses *agape*. These facts seem to indicate that Paul was the first person in history to use the word extensively.

Paul does not copy his uses of *agape* from any previous source. His writings contain only four instances of obvious dependence upon the Old Testament: Romans 9:25 to 26, 9:13, 13:9, and Galatians 5:14. These latter two appear to be dependent upon the teaching of Christ. Furthermore, these four references involve *agapao* rather than *agape*. Nor is Paul dependent upon other New Testament sources. In the only New Testament usage of *agape* before any writings of Paul, the content is vague: "the love of many shall wax cold." Luke contains the word once, but since he was a companion of Paul, his use reflects that of his teacher. Thus, Paul's primary source for his use of *agape* was his own original thinking plus infallible guidance from the Holy Spirit. This combination produced an entirely new content for the word: "giving oneself as a deliberate choice for the highest good."This content is in harmony with every occurrence of the word in the writings of Paul and in those Biblical authors who wrote after him. The only possible exception in the entire New Testament is the verse previously mentioned, Matthew 24:12, which was penned before any writings of Paul and which was used by Christ in a vague sense.

# The Sovereignty of God's Agape

Paul clearly shows God's *agape* to be sovereign: that is, God loves whom He pleases, when He pleases, in the manner He pleases, producing the results which He alone determines. An example which clearly illustrates this point occurs in the most familiar passage of Scripture: "For God so loved the world that He gave..." Further evidence that God's *agape* is sovereign occurs in Romans 5:6-8 and 10. Contrary to the love which has its source in man, divine love was demonstrated for the ungodly, not the righteous but for sinners who were God's enemies. According to human standards, this love is unnatural and so requires a sovereign choice.

Ephesians 2 comments on the same theme: because of His love, God quickened the spiritually dead Gentiles, putting them in Christ Jesus, and giving to them citizenship with the saints of the household of God.

The sovereignty of God's *agape*, however, does not imply that God expects or desires no response on the part of the objects. Rather, the opposite is true. The classic statement on the sovereignty of God's *agape* occurs in Romans 8:35-39, which states that, though *agape* expects a response from man, it is not dependent upon any response.

> "Who shall separate us from the love of Christ? Shall tribulation, or distress, or persecution, or famine, or nakedness, or peril, or sword? As it is written: For Your sake we are killed all day long; We are accounted as sheep for the

slaughter.' Yet in all these things we are more than conquerors through Him who loved us. For I am persuaded that neither death nor life, nor angels, nor principalities, nor powers, nor things present, nor things to come, nor height, nor depth, nor any other created thing shall be able to separate us from the love of God, which is in Christ Jesus our Lord."

# The Walk of Agape

PAUL SHOWS *AGAPE* TO BE A CONSTANT ATTITUDE of the mind and heart that commands Christians to always walk in love (Ephesians 5:2). As a constant attitude, it becomes a strong motivation force, in which the Christian should continually abound, being rooted and grounded in it.

Paul makes it clear that though a Christian has been saved by grace apart from works, yet he is "created in Christ Jesus for good works, which God prepared beforehand that he should walk in them" (Ephesians 2:10). God does not save merely for the sake of saving, but He has a purpose for each of His actions. He saves a person in order that He might enable that person to produce good works, the production of which becomes his vocation. Paul delineates specifically this vocation in the last three chapters of Ephesians. He describes the end of this vocation as resulting in a perfect man, unto the measure of the stature of the fullness of Christ; that is, the person becomes "conformed to the image of His Son" (Romans 8:29). When a Christian walks in love, he produces those characteristics and works which are in harmony with the nature of God and for which God has saved him (Galatians 5:22-23). When these are perfected, that person then conforms to the image of Christ and fulfills the purpose for which he was created (I John 3:3).

No human, however, can reproduce the character of Christ in his own life and through his own strength, but only as he yields to the Spirit of God (Ephesians 5:18). In such a state the Holy Spirit so controls the person that Paul can say, "For it is God who works in you both to will and to do of His good pleasure" (Philippians 2:13). Furthermore, Paul speaks of such Godlike characteristics as "the fruit of the Spirit" (Galatians 5:22).

Because of its value, some would counterfeit *agape*. They attempt to show themselves as possessing characteristics that they do not have. They lie, scheme, cheat, and steal, yet show to others the appearance of extreme love. Paul warns against such love and calls it hypocritical (Romans 12:9). He points to Christ as the supreme example of genuine and sincere *agape* who, "though he was rich, yet for your sakes He became poor, that you through His poverty might be become rich" (II Corinthians 8:9).

# The Value of Agape

PAUL SHOWS *AGAPE* TO POSSESS SUPREME VALUE AND benefit. The cost is little when compared to the gain involved by acquiring it. Almost in every one of his Epistles, he shows at least one way in which it benefits the person possessing it.

- In Romans, it provides salvation.

- In I Corinthians, it builds up in contrast to knowledge which puffs up.

- In II Corinthians, it provides motivation for the Lord's work.

- In Galatians, it directs service toward one another.

- In Ephesians, it provides predestination.

- In Philippians, it comforts.

- In Colossians, it knits together.

- In I Thessalonians, it acts as a shield.

- In II Thessalonians, it motivates the Lord in providing salvation from His wrath.

- In II Timothy, it extinguishes fear.

- In Philemon, it brings joy and consolation.

Paul puts *agape* and faith in the same context at least eighteen times. Some of these occurrences are simply a list of virtues, but others show a definite relationship between the two. In Galatians 5:16-21 and 5:22-23, Paul contrasts the works of the flesh with the fruit of the Spirit. He then lists the fruit of the Spirit: love (*agape*), joy, peace, longsuffering, kindness, goodness, faithfulness, gentleness, self-control. Every Christian lives in the Spirit (verse 25), that is, the Holy Spirit is the means for the believer's spiritual existence, but he should also "walk in the Spirit." This last phrase likewise is considered a use of the instrumental case in Greek, giving the sense "by means of" the Spirit. Only as the Holy Spirit controls the life of the individual can that person produce the Spirit's fruit. And the first in the list of fruits is *agape*.

In the first chapter of Genesis, God established a natural law that every living thing would bring forth after its kind (Genesis 1:24). This law is repeated in the New Testament. Paul says that whatsoever a man sows, that he will also reap (Galatians 6:7). As the fruit of any living thing reflects the identity and character of its parent, so the fruit of the Spirit must reflect the character of God. Since God constitutes the highest good, these fruits of the Spirit, being characteristics of God, reflect God. Since God is *agape*, He desires the production of these characteristics. God, by means of the Holy Spirit, produces these characteristics in man. The fruit of the Spirit, therefore, is the result of God's *agape* for the Christian.

*Agape* occurs first in the list of the fruit of the Spirit. This occurrence should be expected since everything brings forth "after its own kind." God's *agape*, by means of the Holy Spirit, produces *agape* in the Christian. Looking at this verse from such a viewpoint gives theological grounds to those who would place a colon after the word *agape* and make the remaining list to be component parts. However, the only literary ground for doing so comes from the singular form of the word "fruit." Each item of the list is always present in every life where *agape* occurs and is related to it. Both joy and peace constitute the inward results from having the highest directive in life, which is to be like Christ. On the other hand, longsuffering, kindness, goodness, faithfulness, and gentleness constitute both the outward and the upward effects, that is, they show how a person relates to God and to others.

# First Corinthians Thirteen

SEVERAL THINGS NEED TO BE NOTED IN THIS chapter. The first is that the possession of *agape* is better than the possession of any or all of the spiritual gifts that are mentioned in the previous chapter. Paul calls *agape* "a more excellent way." As such, *agape* does not constitute a goal in itself, but it is a way or a means to a goal. This idea finds support in several of the characteristics of *agape*, such as longsuffering, which in verse four implies taking the long view, as well as "bears all things, believes all things, hopes all things, endures all things" (verse 7). This latter verse cannot be understood by itself, for it would imply that everyone possessing *agape* would believe all lies and endure all sin. Evidence abounds to show that this is not so. *Agape* bears all things, believes all things, hopes all things, and endures all things in relationship to its goal. Thus, the farmer bears the task of instructing his son in the art of farming and of the cost from his son's mistakes, yet he believes that his son is able to learn and is making progress. He hopes that the day will come when his son will be a good farmer. All the while, the father endures the gripes and complaints voiced by one who would rather spend his time playing instead of working. Even so, *agape* keeps its eye on the goal of becoming Christlike while enduring temporary disappointments.

A person not possessing *agape* is worthless, and consequently, each of the three suppositions of the first three verses demonstrates this fact. In verse one communication without *agape* is just noise. In verse two spiritual gifts without *agape* leave a person with no value. In verse three even to give supreme sacrifice, to give one's body to be burned when not motivated by *agape*, adds no value to the person.

*Agape* does not keep company with sin. "Love does not envy; love does not parade itself, is not puffed up; does not behave rudely, does not seek her own, is not provoked, thinks no evil; does not rejoice in iniquity" (verses 4-6). Most of these characteristics have to do with pride and its manifestation. *Agape* denies self, parts company with sin, maintains a standard, and rejoices in and with the truth. Truth rejoices only when its opponent, iniquity, suffers defeat. Sin, which is only selfishness in one form or another, is the exact opposite of *agape*.

*Agape* never fails. It will continue throughout eternity, though some spiritual gifts are only temporary. It never fails because it is perfect, enjoys perfection, and desires the production of perfection. It continually labors to conform each one who possesses it to the image of Christ, and when perfection comes, that which is in part shall be done away.

# Agape and the Epistles of Hebrews,
# I and II Peter, and Jude

HEBREWS. THE AUTHOR OF THIS BOOK USES BOTH *agape* and *agapao* twice. Each reference to *agape* connects it with good works. In the first reference, love is directed to God's name and manifests itself through ministry to the saints. In the second reference, Christians are given the responsibility to encourage other Christians to acquire *agape* and to display good works. Both references seem to imply that the good works are the result of possessing *agape*.

The two uses of *agapao* are unique for this word in the New Testament. The first use in 1:9 is quoted from Psalm 45:7 and reveals God's love directed towards a quality, righteousness. A similar use of *agapao* occurs in Second Thessalonians 2:10, where love is directed toward truth. Both righteousness and truth characterize the highest good and so harmonize with the definition of *agape* stated previously. The other use of *agapao* states the motive of God in chastening His children (Hebrews 12:6). Though *agape* is not the only kind of love which chastens, it is the only kind of love which demands chastening in a parent-child relationship. In not chastening the child, the indulgent parent does not love his child but is rather motivated by selfishness.

The writer of Hebrews also declares God's *agape* for man when he states who Christ is and what He has done for man's good. He, by Himself, "purged our sins," having suffered on to perfection to become a "merciful and faithful high priest in things pertaining to God, to make propitiation for the sins of the people" (2:17). Now, He bids Christians "to come boldly to the throne of grace to obtain mercy and grace to help in time of need," (4:16). God produces in the lives of Christians that which is well pleasing in His sight in order to make them "complete in every good work" (13:21).

**First Peter.** This Epistle uses the noun, *agape*, three times (in 4:8 twice and once in 5:14) and the verb, *agapao*, four times (1:8, 22; 2:17 and 3:10), though in the latter reference where it is taken from Psalm 34, it simply means desire. Love for fellow Christians takes a prominent place in the other references and is commanded. Peter states the reason for the concept by saying that *agape* continually "covers a multitude of sins." The forgiveness of sins by God does not enter the context here. Peter simply states in his own words Paul's statement, showing that *agape* "bears all things, believes all things, hopes all things, endures all things" (I Corinthians 13:7). The Christian who possesses *agape* for his fellow Christians should express such a love toward them. In II Corinthians 12:12, Paul admonishes Christians to "greet one another with a holy kiss." In the American culture of today, a handshake, a pat on the shoulder, or a hug would be appropriate.

Peter also mentions love for Jesus Christ even though the recipients of his Epistle had not seen Him (1:8). Their *agape* along with their faith produced a heart "rejoicing with joy unspeakable and full of glory" because to them the Lord Jesus was precious (2:6). Such a love readily calls forth the praises of Him who hath called them out of darkness into light (2:9). Christ deserves the love of Christians since He Himself bore their "sins in his own body on the tree," (2:24), suffering for sins, "the just for the unjust" (3:18). In this, He has become an example to all Christians that they should follow His steps (2:21).

**II Peter.** The concept of *agape* occurs seldom in this Epistle and the word *agape* occurs only once (1:7). Here, Christians are commanded to supply *agape* in their brotherly love. *Agape,* along with several other virtues, enables Christians to have a full knowledge of Jesus Christ and to be fruitful in their lives (1:8).

**Jude.** The noun *agape* occurs first in verse 2, where it is used with mercy and peace. The second occurrence, however, is unique in that it is the only instance in the New Testament of the plural form (verse 12). The Authorized version translates it "feasts of charity," which probably best conforms to the author's intention. The third reference to *agape* in Jude commands Christians to keep themselves in the love of God (verse 21). This verse does not contradict the truth expressed by Paul, who says in Romans 8 that nothing can separate the Christian from the love of God. Paul is looking at the ultimate end for the Christian. Although the Christian may occasionally sin and be temporarily separated in fellowship from God, still God continues to work in his life and to chastise him for his sin in order that ultimately, he may be conformed to the image of Christ. Jude looks at the Christian's responsibility from day-to-day and tells him not to sin and be separated in fellowship from God, but to stay in the place where he can constantly experience God's love.

# Agape in the Writings of John

JOHN IS KNOWN AS THE APOSTLE OF LOVE; yet he uses the two words *agape* (30 times) and *agapao* (71 times) fewer times than does Paul. Also, his use of the word more readily accords with earlier usage in that he predominantly uses the verb rather than the noun.

# The Transmission of Agape

GOD, WHO IS THE SOURCE OF ALL *AGAPE*, transmits or communicates His love to man. He communicates His love to the world potentially so that it is available to anyone and everyone who believes. John 3:16, probably the best-known verse in the Bible, declares that "God so loved the world, that He gave His only begotten Son, that whosoever believes in Him should not perish, but have everlasting life." The first truth to note in this verse is the result of *agape*: God gave. *Agape* always produces action for the benefit of its object. Usually this action is in the form of giving. Thus, the Samaritan, having *agape* for his neighbor, aided the man who had fallen among thieves by giving sacrificially. This *agape*, however, may not always appear beneficial as it might be in the form of chastening, and the object of the *agape* does not have the prerogative to judge. The second factor is the expense of *agape*. The cost was high. God, having *agape*, could not consider His own comfort first, but gave everything required, even that which was most dear to Him, His only begotten Son. The third factor is the limit to *agape*. Though one often thinks of God's *agape* as being infinite, yet He limited the *agape* to His Son. Those who refuse this gift are left to perish. Fourth is the response to *agape*. Although God did not expect payment of any sort, He did expect a response from the object of his *agape*. He required that a person believe. Only such persons will have everlasting life and not perish. The fifth factor is the result involved. Those who respond with faith to God's *agape* receive everlasting life. As one continues to study the nature of *agape* and to apply it to his life, he must keep these five factors in mind. To eliminate even one will cause a deficiency in either one's life, one's theology, or both.

The Christian actually has the privilege of receiving God's *agape*, and this love becomes in him a moral force, issuing in love for the brethren, in self-sacrifice, and in love toward God. Thus, the Christian not only shares the life of Christ but also the love of Christ. Although Paul looks at this love in the life of a Christian from the divine side as the fruit of the Spirit, John views it from the human standpoint of abiding in Christ as the branch abides in the vine (John 15:4-10).

# The Response to God's Agape

OBEDIENCE. ALTHOUGH JOHN MENTIONS THAT A CHRISTIAN RESPONDS to God's love with love for God, he places a stronger emphasis upon the fact that a pure life and an obedient attitude will follow if one has *agape*. This is true in both his Gospel and his first Epistle: "If you love me, keep my commandments" (John 14:15); "He who has my commandments, and keeps them, it is he who loves me" (John 14:21); "He who does not love Me does not keep my words" (John 14:24); "But whoever keeps His word, truly the love of God is perfected in him" (I John 2:5). "For this is the love of God, that we keep His commandments" (I John 5:3). John begins the third chapter of his first Epistle by saying, "Behold, what manner of love the Father has bestowed upon us" (I John 3:1); and quickly follows it up with, "And every man that has this hope in him purifies himself, even as He is pure" (I John 3:3). Several verses later he says, "Whoever abides in Him sins not" (I John 3:6). "Whoever is born of God does not commit sin" (verse 9); and "In this the children of God are manifest, and the children of the devil: whoever does not practice righteousness is not of God, neither he who does not love his brother" (verse 10). Many other instances can be cited, but this is sufficient to demonstrate that *agape* in the heart produces obedience in the life.

**Love for the Brethren.** Only Christianity makes *agape* its badge. "By this all will know that you are my disciples..." (John 13:35). It is the Western world that has provided the freedom by which Christianity has been able to thrive and to manifest this badge through the centuries.

Since love for the brethren should be patterned after Christ's love, sacrifice describes its nature. A person who does not lay down his life for the brethren, that is, for those who are God's children and who manifest a God-like character, does not love God. In fact, it is the possession of *agape* for the brethren that indicates a person has been saved (I John 3:14).

# The Results of Agape

SONSHIP. JOHN CLEARLY STATES THAT SONSHIP IS A result of God's love to the Christian: "Behold, what manner of love the father has bestowed on us, that we should be called the children of God…" (I John 3:1). I John 4:7 states that every son of God loves as God loves.

**Fellowship**. John also places a strong emphasis upon fellowship in both his Gospel and his first Epistle. No better passages could be cited from his Gospel than John 15: 4, 5, 7, 9, and 10.

"Abide in Me and I in you. As the branch cannot bear fruit of itself, unless it abides in the vine; neither can you, unless you abide in Me. I am the Vine, you are the branches; He who abides in Me, and I in him, bears much fruit: for without Me you can do nothing… if you abide in Me, and My words abide in you, you will ask what you desire, and it shall be done for you… as the Father loved Me, I also have loved you: abide in My love. If you keep my commandments, you will abide in My love; just as I have kept my Father's commandments and abide in His love."

Fellowship is based on mutual agreement, and so the prophet Amos asked, "Can two walk together, unless they be agreed?" (Amos 3:3). Paul asked the question, which expects a negative answer, when he says, "For what fellowship has righteousness with unrighteousness?" (II Corinthians 6:14). In the verses quoted above, John shows that to have fellowship with God, one must be in agreement with and be submissive to Him. I John 1:3-7 especially relates fellowship to the matter of sin, for, "If we say that we have fellowship with Him, and walk in darkness, we lie, and do not practice the truth" (I John 1:6). Fellowship with God is thus directly related to agreement with God. An obedient lifestyle is directly related to *agape*, for "if you keep My commandments, you shall abide in My love; even as I have kept my Father's commandments, and abide in His love." (John 15:10) *Agape* in the heart produces obedience in the life, which in turn permits fellowship with God.

God has *agape* for the whole world, yet the whole world is not in fellowship with Him. Those who walk in darkness are not in fellowship, and "...he who believes not is condemned already..." (John 3:18). The remedy for broken fellowship is confession of sins for "if we confess our sins, He is faithful and just to forgive us our sins and to cleanse us from all unrighteousness" (I John 1:9).

Yet, no one has had perfect, continuous fellowship with the Father except Jesus Christ (John 15:9-10). The thought of "no man hath seen God at any time," implies a continuous beholding that has its counterpart in abiding fellowship. The person who has *agape* has continuous fellowship, for *agape* dwells in him in the person of the Holy Spirit.

There are those churches, however, that lose their first *agape* and are put in a precarious position (Revelation 2:4). If *agape* unites, the loss of *agape* naturally results in estrangement and the removal of "your candlestick from its place" (Revelation 2:5). The only possible remedy demands repentance before fellowship and usefulness can be restored.

**Confidence**. Love for one another involves mutual giving to that other, but fear means the shrinking from one another. Therefore, love and fear are not compatible. A person who possesses *agape* for God cannot fear God except reverentially, but still have confidence in Him and "boldness in the day of judgment" (I John 4:17). "There is no fear in love; but perfect love casts out fear: because fear involves torment. But he who fears has not been made perfect in love" (I John 4:18).

# The Perversion of Agape

John commands the Christian not to love the world: "Do not love the world or the things in the world. If anyone loves the world, the love of the Father is not in him. For all that *is* in the world—the lust of the flesh, the lust of the eyes, and the pride of life—is not of the Father but is of the world. And the world is passing away, and the lust of it; but he who does the will of God abides forever" (I John 2:15-17).

God forbids the Christian to love the world, and if he should, the *agape* of the Father is not in him. Yet "God so loved the world that He gave His only begotten Son". An apparent contradiction exists: God loved the world but forbids His children to do so. If God hates only the institutions and evil of men, why does His wrath abide on the persons themselves rather than simply on their institutions and evil? Man was born in sin and possesses a sinful nature, and this sinful condition makes the separation between the person and his sin an impossibility. His sins and institutions result only because he is basically a sinner.

And just what is sin? The common definition that we all think about but never put into words is this: "all the bad things that everybody else does." Sometimes we even whitewash some sin by labels such as, "little white lies" or ignorance or mistakes, or… Or… God informs us quite clearly in Genesis chapter three where we have the story of man's first sin. The serpent is very cunning and begins his conversation with Eve by implying that God has given them an unreasonable command: "Has God indeed said…" Next, he lies by saying that God did not speak the truth: "You will not surely die." Then he points out to Eve the good things about the tree, climaxing the conversation by saying, "When you eat this fruit, your eyes will be opened and you will be like God, knowing good and evil." In other words, "God has brainwashed you. You don't need God to tell you right from wrong. You can decide for yourself. Be your own god." The result was that Eve removed God from her life so she could run things herself. The heart of sin is the enthronement of oneself over God. This is selfishness in all its forms. It is the exact opposite of *agape*.

# The Relationship of Agape to Mercy, Grace, and Faith

Mercy, grace, faith, and *agape* should not be confused. In Ephesians 2:4, 5, and 8 the four words appear in the same context: "But God, who is rich in mercy, because of His great love with which He loved us, even when we were dead in trespasses, made us alive together with Christ (by grace you have been saved), … For by grace you have been saved through faith, and that not of yourselves; it is the gift of God." Other examples of at least two of these words appearing in the same context are I Timothy 1:2, Titus 1:4, Hebrews 4:16, II Timothy 1:2, II John 3, and Jude 2.

**Mercy.** Mercy is used of men as well as of God. Both the beatitude recorded by Matthew, "Blessed are the merciful: for they shall obtain mercy" (Matthew 5:7), and that recorded by Luke, "Therefore be merciful, just as your Father also is merciful (Luke 6:36) demonstrate this comparison. Of the former, Christ says mercy is withholding punishment upon an adversary, while in the latter, mercy is compassion to help the weak, the sick, and the poor or someone else in need. Psalm 6:2 pleads, "Have mercy on me, O LORD, for I am weak; O LORD, heal me, for my bones are troubled" (Psalm 6:2). In the New Testament, several instances occurred where the Lord was asked to have mercy upon persons with some physical handicap or sickness. The common belief existed that sickness was the judgment of God upon the individual for some sin. The Lord as the Son of David was asked to set aside a judgment and use His healing power to deliver the victim from his misery. Mercy, therefore, appears to be the willingness of God to set aside judgments which a person has incurred, whether physical or spiritual, to relieve one of his misery.

In Ephesians two, where the four words appear together, Paul pictures the character of each unsaved person as walking according to the course of this world, fulfilling the desires of the flesh and of the mind, and being by nature children of wrath. Verse four begins with the word of contrast, "but". Though the natural person is a child of wrath, God is rich in mercy and is willing to set aside the judgment. However, God's mercy does not overlook sin; rather, it finds a remedy for it. His mercy is exercised because of His great *agape*. Mercy is God's *agape* in action to relieve the misery from the recipient.

**Grace.** What then is "Grace"? The word occurs in the Greek text of the Bible over one hundred and seventy times. It has a vast number of uses in secular Greek but only Biblical uses will concern us here. One stands out far above the others. This is set forth very well by J. Gresham Machen. He comments that grace is:

> *"the centre of the Christian religion—the absolutely undeserved and sovereign grace of God, saving sinful men by the gift of Christ upon the cross. Condemnation comes by merit; salvation comes only by grace; condemnation is earned by man; salvation is given by God. The fact of the grace of God runs through the New Testament like a golden thread; indeed for it the New Testament exists. It is found in the words which Jesus spoke in the days of His flesh, as in the parables of the servant coming in from the field and of the laborers in the vineyard; it is found more fully set forth after the redeeming work was done, after the Lord had uttered His triumphant "It is finished" upon the cross. Everywhere the basis of the New Testament is the same—the mysterious, incalculable, wondrous, grace of God. "The wages of sin is death, but the gift of God is eternal life through Jesus Christ our Lord."*

The main emphasis of the word "grace" is that salvation comes as a gift to us. It is entirely without cost. It is unmerited. Salvation comes by grace, and so is absolutely free. Condemnation comes by merit, and so has been earned.

**Faith.** Faith is mentioned over and over again in the New Testament. There is little faith and great faith. It can fail; it can increase, it can be denied. It makes whole, purifies the heart, and brings propitiation, justification and righteousness. It is never attributed to the Lord Jesus, nor to God. Only human beings possess it. Romans 3:3 is a possible exception, but the New King James Bible translates the Greek word, πίστις in this instance as "faithfulness." It says, "For what if some did not believe? Will this unbelief make the faithfulness of God without effect?" Faith, however, requires an object, but in this instance, it does not. New Testament faith has as its object both Jesus Christ and God.

The child of God is to live by faith (Romans 1:17) which comes from the Word of God. (Romans 10:17) and is manifested by good works (James 2:18).

Now let us compare the four words. *Agape* is what motivates God: His deliberate choice and commitment to give Himself for the good of the other. Mercy emphasizes our helplessness to save ourselves. Grace emphasizes the freeness of the salvation that God provides. Faith is the means that is required to receive it. We must trust Him. Regarding salvation: *agape* supplies; **grace** applies; **faith** relies.

Another way of comparison is: *Agape* is giving oneself for the good of another. **Mercy** is one way agape functions giving to those who cannot pay. **Grace** is the attitude of God looking for ways to give so that the recipient receives the gift at no cost to himself. **Faith** is the attitude of trust necessary to receive God's gifts of grace.

# Conclusion

WE NOW COME TO THE CONCLUSION AND ANSWER the question that got my attention when I first became a Christian as a teenager. How can love which is an emotion be commanded? In answer, the *agape* love that is commanded is not an emotion, but a conscious, deliberate action or choice that is made possible only after a person has made the choice to give himself to God.

Since God's most basic characteristic is *agape* and God has created us in His own image and is continuing to form us into that image *agape* should be a part of us if not <u>our</u> basic characteristic. To really have a meaningful and joyful life, we must be what God has made us to be. We must be giving ourselves for the good of the other. Jesus said, "It is more blessed to give than to receive" (Acts 20:35). We all question this. We arrive on planet Earth wanting to get and we never seem to have enough. Therefore, we are never satisfied and always want more. Our houses are filled with things and many rent additional storage space because we want. Agape love tells us to give and give and give and give. A farm tractor was not made to take a family to a beach in Florida for a vacation. It does best by helping a farmer in his fields. Even so, we were not made to get and get but rather to give and to give of ourselves and so image God in His basic characteristic. Then and only then will we have a satisfying life.

Lightning Source UK Ltd.
Milton Keynes UK
UKHW042303150223
417099UK00006B/10

9 781950 947546